Contents

About canals	4
Canals in the past	6
Canal structures	8
Materials	10
Going up and down	12
Designing canals	14
Site preparation	16
Liners and locks	18
Canals in use	20
Ships in the desert	22
The Erie Canal	24
Canal disasters	26
Canal facts	28
Glossary	30
Index	32

Words appearing in the text in bold, **like this**, are explained in the Glossary.

About canals

Any stretch of water that boats and ships (called craft) use to travel inland from the sea is called a waterway. Unlike a stream or river, a canal is an artificial waterway, made by digging a channel in the ground and filling it with water.

The Panama Canal is one of the world's greatest engineering feats. It cuts the journey from the Atlantic to the Pacific by 15,000 kilometres (9.322 miles).

A canal is made up of different structures. A structure is a thing that resists a push or pull. The channel of a canal is a structure because it supports the huge weight of water in the canal. Other structures such as tunnels and bridges (**aqueducts**) carry canals over valleys, roads and railways.

Building a canal is an enormous **engineering** job. Millions of tonnes of earth and rock are dug up to make the channel, and dozens of **locks**, bridges and aqueducts are constructed from concrete and steel. So why do we build canals? Are there different types of canal? How are they built? Are special materials or machinery needed?

Why do we build canals?

The main job of a canal is to transport goods. Canal travel is much slower than road or rail travel, but a big canal **barge** can carry 2000 tonnes of cargo – as much as 50 trucks. So canals are good for transporting 'bulk' goods, such as coal, ore, grain and timber, which do not need to be moved quickly. They are important in North America, northern Europe and parts of Asia.

Locks are like steps for craft such as barges to move up and down hill.

Most canals are barge canals, and are part of larger waterway networks that link inland cities, industrial areas and ports.
The giants of the canal world are ship canals. They allow huge ocean-going ships to reach inland cities, or take a short cut between two seas or oceans. Not all canals are for transport. Canals are also built to carry water from place to place, for water supply, **irrigation** and drainage.

FACTS ✛ It's a canal world record!

- Longest canal: Grand Canal, China – 1,747 kilometres (1,085 miles).
- Deepest canal: Suez Canal, Egypt – 19.5 metres (64 feet).
- Largest lock: Berendrecht Lock, Antwerp, Belgium – 500 metres (1,640 feet) long; 68 metres (223 feet) wide.

Canals in the past

The first canals were probably built more than 4,000 years ago by ancient civilizations that existed in the **Middle East**. Most of these canals carried river water to fields for **irrigation**, and to cities for drinking. A few were for boats. All the digging was done by hand. Imagine how long they took to build!

The Chinese started building canals in about the 3rd century BC to link large rivers, such as the Yangtze, to cities. Boats carried grain from the fertile plains of the south to the busy cities of the north. Between 400 BC and 100 BC, in northern Europe, the Romans built canals as part of a transport system that carried soldiers, food and other supplies to their huge army.

Canal building boom

Canal networks began to grow rapidly in the 17th century. Among the first canals was the Canal du Midi in southern France, linking the Atlantic Ocean and Mediterranean Sea. The 270-kilometre (170-mile) canal included 100 **locks**, a tunnel and three **aqueducts**. It took 26 years to build.

Barges travelling on China's Grand Canal – the world's oldest working canal.

Coal and crops

Narrow boats working through locks on the Regent's Canal in London in 1827.

In the 18th and 19th centuries, many more canals were built in Europe and North America. The canals were the only way of moving heavy cargo, and they were vital for the development of industries during the **Industrial Revolution**. They brought fuel and raw materials such as coal and timber to factories, and carried goods such as furniture away. **Barges** also carried crops from the countryside to the growing cities.

In North America and Britain the railways had taken most of the canals' trade by the end of the 19th century. Elsewhere, canals are still important. The great ship canals, such as the Suez Canal and Panama Canal, shorten the world's sea routes.

FACTS ✛ Amazing canals of the past

- The Nahrawan, built in **Mesopotamia** more than 5,000 years ago, was 321 kilometres (200 miles) long and 120 metres (400 feet) wide.
- The **Assyrian** king Sennacherib built an 80-kilometre (50 mile) water-supply canal lined in stone in the 7th century BC.
- China's 1,747-kilometre (1,085-mile) Grand Canal was started in AD 607.
- About 5.5 million slave workers built the first section of the Grand Canal in China. Two million died because of the terrible conditions.

7

Canal structures

For most of its length, a canal is a channel in the ground that is filled with water. Its simple structure keeps the water in the channel and stops the **banks** collapsing. Other structures, such as **locks** and **aqueducts**, keep the channel level or carry craft from one level to another.

Channel shapes

The cross-section of a canal channel – the shape you would see if you sliced across a canal and looked at the end – is normally shaped like a **trapezium**. The channel is wider at the top than at the **bed**, and has sloping banks.

Strong sides

Most canal channels have a lining on the bed and the banks. The lining does three jobs. It stops water leaking out of the channel, it supports the banks, and it protects the banks from being **eroded** by the water in the channel.

Where vessels need to tie up at the side of the canal, the banks need to be **vertical** rather than sloping. Here, they are supported by very strong concrete or steel columns or plates, sometimes interlocking along their edges.

These cross-sections show a canal's trapezium shape in the main channel (left), and its rectangular shape in a lock (right).

Locking in water

Canal locks are made up of concrete or stone side walls that hold up the ground at each side of the lock, and gates at each end. The greater the difference between the water levels inside and outside the lock, the bigger the push on the gates. For example, if the difference is 5 metres (16 feet), the pressure on the base of the gate is 100,000 newtons per square metre (360,000 newtons per square foot). That's the same as an elephant sitting in an armchair!

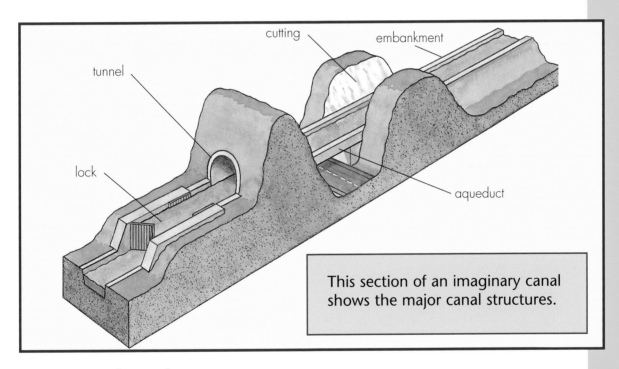

This section of an imaginary canal shows the major canal structures.

Over and under

Where a canal needs to cross a steep-sided valley or go through a range of hills, aqueducts and tunnels are needed to keep the channel level. Aqueducts are similar to road bridges, but they need to be stronger to support the huge weight of the water in the channel. Modern aqueducts are made up of a channel supported by concrete or steel beams. **Cuttings** and **embankments** are also made to take canals through hilly areas.

Materials

A canal will only stay watertight if **engineers** use the right materials for the channel lining. In some places, canals go through solid rock that is waterproof, so no lining is needed. Waterproof lining materials include clay, **bitumen** and **polythene**. A canal's **banks** and **bed** are protected from the wash of boats with gravel, rubble, rocks, or reeds. Some canals have a thick concrete lining covered with bitumen. Other canal structures, such as **locks** and **aqueducts**, use the two most common construction materials – concrete and steel.

Mixing concrete

Concrete is an important construction material because it is cheap and very strong. The ingredients of concrete are **cement**, water and aggregate, which is made up of sand and gravel. When the ingredients are first mixed, the concrete is runny. As the cement and water react together, the mixture gradually hardens to make a solid that holds the aggregate together. Normal concrete takes several hours to harden and about a month to reach its maximum strength.

TRY THIS

Waterproof channels

Fill a large old tray with sand and smooth the surface. Dig a model canal channel about 10 centimetres (4 inches) wide in the sand.
Pour water into the channel.
What happens to the water?
Now try waterproofing the channel with different materials, such as plastic food wrapping, and then fill it again.

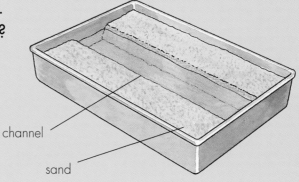

channel

sand

Uncrushable

Concrete is so strong that a mug-sized piece of concrete could support a 30-tonne truck. It can easily be shaped by pouring it into moulds before it sets. **Precast concrete** is set in moulds in a factory to make concrete pieces. These pieces are then taken to the construction site. **In situ** concrete is concrete that is set on site. Canal builders might use precast concrete sections for aqueducts, and *in situ* concrete to build watertight linings and lock walls.

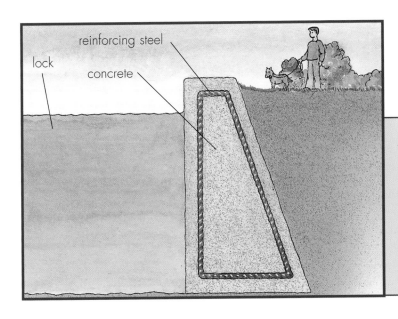

A simple reinforced concrete lock wall. It is thicker at the base to keep it stable.

Super-strong steel

Steel is an **alloy** made mostly of iron. It is used to make lock gates and protective channel linings. Concrete is only strong when you try to squash it. If you try to stretch it, it cracks quite easily. Steel is immensely strong even when stretched. For example, a steel cable as thick as your finger could lift a 30-tonne truck. So where part of a structure made from concrete will be stretched, steel is added. This new material, made up of concrete and steel bars, is called **reinforced concrete**.

11

Going up and down

Gates at each end

If a canal has to go up or down a hill, **locks** are used. A single lock consists of a short section of canal with a set of opening gates at each end. The water level is raised by letting water into the lock, normally from the canal above. This is done by opening **sluice gates** either in the gates themselves or in pipes leading from the canal to the lock. The water level is lowered by letting water out, normally into the canal below.

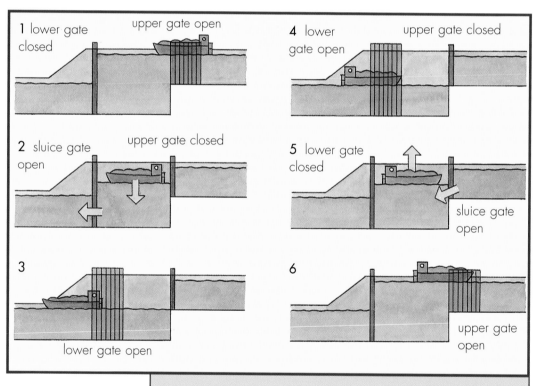

This shows how a boat moves downhill through a lock (1, 2, 3), or uphill (4, 5, 6).

Record-holders

On the Panama Canal each lock is three times as long as a soccer pitch, as deep as a ten-storey building and would take more than a year to fill from a bath tap!

Lock staircases

A single lock is like a step or single stair. It can only raise or lower a craft a certain distance. Very deep locks are difficult and costly to build, so to get up or down a long hill, several locks are often built end to end, making a lock staircase. The longest staircases have dozens of locks, which can take hours to travel through.

Boats in tubs

An **inclined plane** carries craft up and down the hill in enormous containers of water, as big as swimming pools, which roll on railway tracks. Canal lifts raise or lower a craft up and down **vertically** in containers of water.

A barge moves downhill on an inclined plane on the Marne-Rhine Canal in France.

TRY THIS

Mitre gates

Cut a piece of stiff card 10 centimetres (4 inches) square. Lay it between two heavy books placed about 8 centimetres (3 inches) apart. If you press lightly in the middle, the card will bend. Now fold it card into a V-shape and place it between the books. Press again. The bend makes it stronger. Large locks have pairs of mitre gates that meet at an angle and resist the push of water better than flat gates.

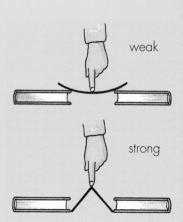

weak

strong

Designing canals

Today, it is normally a government organization that decides to build a canal, perhaps because they want a new link in a transport network. A consulting **engineer** then oversees the design and construction of the canal.

Which way?

Planning a route for a canal is more difficult than for a road or railway because the canal has to stay level. The route has to avoid hills and valleys as far as possible because going over them means building expensive **aqueducts**, tunnels and **locks**. But the route cannot be too long or too winding.

Many old canals twisted and turned, following the contours of the hills to save expensive **cuttings**, tunnels and bridges.

Engineers will look at several possible routes and decide which is best. They also dig **boreholes** to look at the earth and rocks along the route. This way we can make sure it will be possible to dig the channel, and see what extra materials will be needed to make it waterproof. Building locks, **inclined planes** and lifts is also avoided when possible because they slow down how quickly craft can move along the canal. Any delay may cost money.

Choosing a channel

The width and depth of a canal channel depends on the size of the craft that are going to use it. The width at the surface is normally made about six times the width of the craft, which leaves space for craft to pass each other. Ship canals need to be much deeper and wider than **barge** canals. The Suez Canal is more than 250 metres (820 feet) across and nearly 20 metres (65 feet) deep.

Locks, aqueducts, and tunnels are also designed if they are needed. So are any new bridges which might be needed to carry roads and railways over the new canal.

TRY THIS

Planning a route

Look at a map of the area where you live that shows the **contours** of the land. Choose two towns on the map and try to work out a route for a canal between the two. Remember that if you follow a contour line, your canal will be level. If you cross contours, your canal will need locks. You could trace or photocopy the map and draw your route on the copy.

Site preparation

Once the route of a canal is decided and the channel and other parts have been designed, construction can begin. Building a canal is an enormous undertaking which can take many years and cost millions. Normally one **engineering** company, called the main contractor, organizes the whole construction job. There are also dozens of smaller companies called sub-contractors, who do special jobs such as tunnelling, **surveying**, or supplying steel.

A new canal could be hundreds of kilometres long, so construction normally starts at one end and carries on to the other end. Careful planning is needed so that machines, materials and workers are all in the right place when they are needed.

This monster earth-moving machine digs canals using massive buckets on a wheel.

Monster machinery

The first stage is to create a level route and dig the channel itself, and create **cuttings** and **embankments**. This involves moving millions of tonnes of soil and rock. Powerful earth-moving machines do most of the work. Scrapers remove a layer of earth as they move, and collect the earth in a skip. Excavators dig down into the ground using a toothed bucket on the end of an arm. Bulldozers push loose earth and rock about. Loaders pick up loose earth and rock and load it into dump trucks. Where solid rock needs to be removed, it is broken up with explosives first. Tunnels are **blasted** with explosives or bored with special machines called moles.

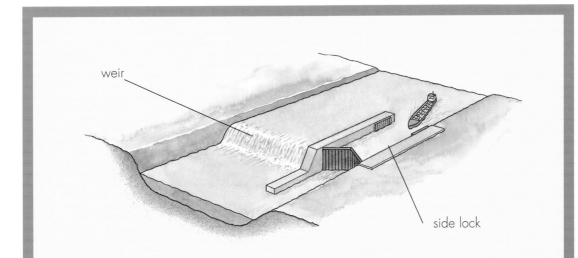

weir

side lock

Navigable rivers

Many waterways are **navigable** rivers. Shallow rivers are made navigable by adding small dams called **weirs**, with short canals with locks around them. This process is called canalization. The river channel itself can be made deeper and wider, and the **banks** can be strengthened. Sharp bends in the river are straightened. This work is done with machines called dragline excavators, which work from the river banks or from floating **barges** in the river.

Liners and locks

Once the earth-moving has been completed, work can start on the channel lining itself. The work normally progresses in sections. Once the earth-moving on a section of canal is complete, the earth-moving machines move on to the next section while the first section is lined.

A new section of the Main-Danube Canal behind the River Danube, in Germany.

Laying a lining

Laying the channel lining is quite a simple process. In some canals gravel or stones are tipped into the channel and spread into a thin layer over the **bed** and **banks**. For a concrete channel lining, concrete is transported to the site in trucks from a concrete-mixing plant. Thousands of truckloads of concrete are needed for every kilometre of canal. On steep banks, the concrete must be kept in place until it sets. When it is dry, a layer of waterproofing is added. Protection for the banks, such as stones or matting covered in **bitumen**, is added. Plants such as reeds are often encouraged to grow near a bank to help protect it.

Thick walls and floors

You can picture a lock as an enormous, watertight, **reinforced concrete** container, with a floor and walls several metres thick. The earth walls are supported by a temporary wall of long **piles** driven deep into the ground. A mould for the concrete is made with wooden sheets or steel plates, called formwork. Reinforcing steel is placed so that it will be encased when the concrete sets. The steel **lock** gates are built in a factory and delivered whole or in sections. They hang on huge hinges in the concrete walls.

FACTS ✛ Building canals

- It took more than 3 million cubic metres (4 million cubic yards) of concrete to build the Panama Canal's huge locks – enough to fill 600 Olympic swimming pools!

- 73 million cubic metres (95 million cubic yards) of earth were dug up to make the Suez Canal. That's enough to fill 50 Olympic stadiums!

The enormous steel lock gates on the Panama Canal are hollow so they float, taking the weight off their hinges.

Canals in use

Using a canal is similar to using a road. There are rules that boats have to follow like a highway code. Speed limits prevent collisions and **erosion** to the **banks**. Craft always keep to the right when passing others coming in the opposite direction. On small canals crews may have to operate **locks** themselves. On larger canals lock keepers operate the locks. They communicate with other lock keepers on the canal so that they know when craft are on the way.

Canal craft

Many different types of craft use canals. Some are small craft such as rowing boats, and some are ocean-going ships. **Barges** are craft designed for use on canals and waterways. They have a shallow **draught**, but are often very wide. Dumb barges are barges without engines that are moved by motorized barges. A train of dumb barges can carry as much cargo as a large ship. They are designed to fit neatly into the locks on the canal they are used on. However, many British locks are only about 2 metres (6.5 feet) wide, and are used by barges called narrow boats.

Dumb barges are moved by a tug along the Mississippi River, USA.

Keep it clear

Canals must be maintained to keep them open to canal traffic. When canals freeze over in winter, ice-breaking craft break the ice. **Sediment** that builds up in the bottom of canals is regularly removed by **dredgers**. If a bank collapses, it must be repaired. The water level has to be kept up, so water may have to be pumped into a canal, or released into it from a **reservoir**.

A "bucket" dredger has a line of buckets on a cable that dig **silt** from the canal bottom.

Lock gates are regularly checked by divers for damage. Every few **decades** gates have to be replaced. This means emptying the water out of the lock and the section of canal next to it. The canal stays closed while the work is done.

Fun on the water

Many old canals are no longer used for cargo traffic, but they make good leisure facilities. People can travel along canals in canoes, rowing boats and cruise boats, walk along the **towpaths**, or fish from the banks. Some canals have special channels that canoeists can use to bypass locks.

Ships in the desert

The Suez Canal is a huge ship canal in Egypt that links the Mediterranean Sea to the Red Sea. It cuts about 5,000 kilometres (3,100 miles) off the route from northern Europe to Asia, and avoids a very long trip around Africa. The Suez Canal is one of the busiest shipping lanes in the world, and is used especially by huge oil tankers sailing from the Persian Gulf to Europe.

The route

The Suez Canal runs almost directly south from Port Said on the Mediterranean Sea to the Gulf of Suez on the Red Sea. It does not take the shortest route between the two seas, but goes through two large lakes that make up about a quarter of its length.

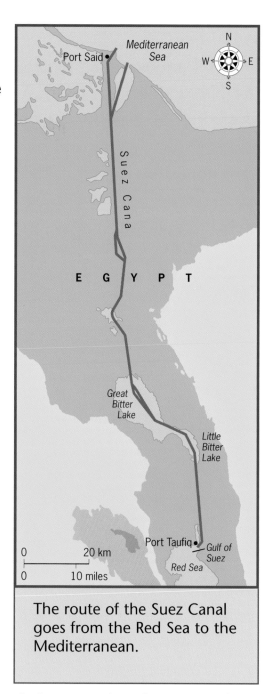

The route of the Suez Canal goes from the Red Sea to the Mediterranean.

The channel is only wide enough for one ship for most of its length, but there are four passing places where ships travelling in opposite directions can pass each other. Ships normally go through the canal in convoys, one behind the other. Each ship is controlled by a local **pilot**, who knows the canal well.

This is a view of the Suez Canal from a freighter waiting its turn to pass into the channel.

The building project

In 1854 a French diplomat called Ferdinand de Lesseps put forward the plan to build the canal. Work started in 1859. Most digging was done with steam-powered shovels and **dredgers** which dug sand and **silt** from the bottom of the canal. The water levels in the Mediterranean and Red Seas are about the same, and the route goes across quite flat land, so no **locks** were needed. The channel was originally 7 metres (23 feet) deep and 58 metres (190 feet) wide, which was big enough for the steamships of the time.

Eventually the Suez Canal had to be widened and deepened to allow for larger ships. In 1954 it was widened to 151 metres (500 feet) with a maximum depth of 15 metres (50 feet). In 1980 it was expanded to 270 metres (890 feet), with a depth of 19.5 metres (64 feet).

The canal also acts as an **irrigation** canal for the towns and farms that have grown up along its length.

FACTS ✣ Suez Canal

- Length: 168 kilometres (104 miles)
- Width at surface: 270 metres (64 feet)
- Depth: 19.5 metres (64 feet)
- Ships per year: 25,000 (40 to 70 per day)
- Transit time: 11–16 hours
- Speed limit: 16 kilometres (10 miles) per hour.

The Erie Canal

Fun on the canal! The Erie Canal is now an important leisure facility.

The Erie Canal was one of the first major canals built in the United States. It connects New York City with the Great Lakes by way of the Hudson River. Buffalo, on Lake Erie, is now a bustling port, but before the canal opened in 1825, it was a lonely outpost that could only be reached by a long journey on horseback. Over the next few **decades** hundreds of thousands of settlers travelled along the Erie Canal and started farms and towns on the lands around the Great Lakes. **Barges** carried their wheat, grain, and timber to New York, and returned with goods from the city. The economic success of the Erie Canal helped to turn New York into a major port.

The Erie Canal is now part of the New York State Barge Canal system, which was opened in 1918. The canal remained an important commercial waterway until the 1950s, when the St Lawrence Seaway opened.

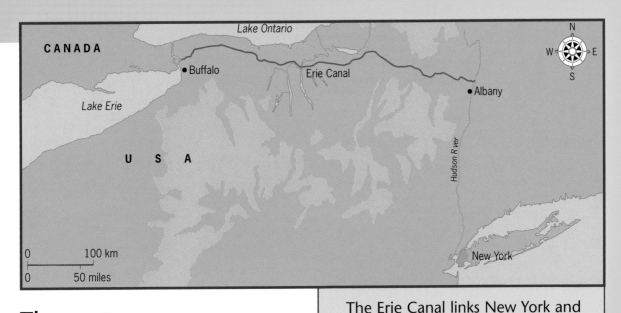

The Erie Canal links New York and the Hudson River to Lake Erie.

The route

The Erie Canal runs 584 kilometres (363 miles) eastward from Buffalo to meet the Hudson River at Albany. The route weaves through a mountain range. Lake Erie is 150 metres (492 feet) above the Hudson River. The canal gains the height with 34 **locks**.

A new challenge

The Erie Canal was proposed by DeWitt Clinton, the governor of New York. The decision to build was made in 1817. Originally there were 83 locks and several long **aqueducts**. Horses carried materials to the site. They also worked machines that pulled up tree stumps, and ploughs that dug the channel. The **engineers** had no experience of canal building. They borrowed ideas from European canal builders, and started in the middle, where digging was easy. They learned by their mistakes. One builder developed a type of waterproof **cement** for the locks.

Creatures from the sea

When the Erie Canal was completed in 1825 it created a route between the Atlantic Ocean and the Great Lakes. It was not only boats that travelled up the canal. A type of **parasite** called the sea lamprey, which attacks fish, gradually spread along the canal and eventually killed millions of fish in the Great Lakes.

Canal disasters

Canals are not complicated structures, and it is rare for anything to go dramatically wrong with them. But there can be problems during construction which slow down the building process. Occasionally there are accidents in canals, and some canals have become unusable for political reasons.

Problems with the Panama Canal

The Panama Canal is a ship canal that crosses the narrow **Isthmus** of Panama in Central America. It links the Atlantic and Pacific Oceans, saving ships a long and stormy journey around Cape Horn.

The Culebra Cut on the Panama Canal took six years to build using steam-powered machinery.

Work on the Panama Canal was started in 1882 by Ferdinand de Lesseps, who had built the Suez Canal. By 1891 he was bankrupt and 20,000 workers had died of tropical diseases, carried by mosquitoes that lived in the swampy areas. In 1903 American **engineers** took over the project. They changed the route so that less digging was needed, but still spent seven years digging a 15-kilometre (9-mile) long **cutting** because of landslides. The canal finally opened in 1914.

The Suez Canal closed

The Suez Canal was closed for the first time in 1956 during a conflict between Israel and Egypt called the Suez Crisis. It was closed again in 1967 during the Arab-Israeli War. It stayed closed until 1975, when many sunken ships were removed and the channel was **dredged**. While it was closed, ships had to spend several extra days sailing round Africa to reach their destinations.

Erie revival

The Erie Canal began to fall into ruin after the 1950s as trains and trucks became more popular forms of transport, and the water became polluted. It was renovated in the 1980s and now provides water, leisure facilities and **hydro-electric power**. **Barges** up to 2,000 tonnes in weight can still use it, but only a few dozen a year do. There are several wildlife parks along its length.

Canal dangers – be careful!

Many canals are used for leisure activities, such as canoeing and fishing. But canals can be dangerous places. The water is often deep and cold, and steep **banks** make it difficult to climb out of the water. **Locks** are especially treacherous. As a lock fills up, the water churns about inside, making it unsafe for small craft such as canoes. **Weirs** are also dangerous because of the swirling wave, called a stopper, at their base. This can trap canoeists and swimmers.

Canal facts

Irrigation and navigable canal systems

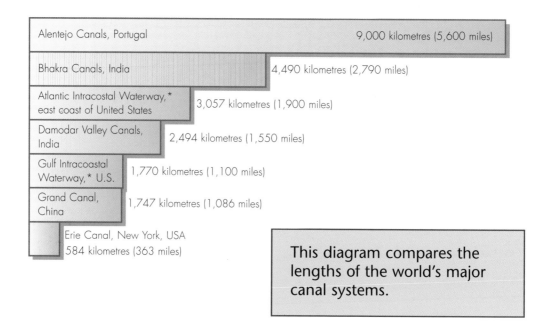

Alentejo Canals, Portugal — 9,000 kilometres (5,600 miles)

Bhakra Canals, India — 4,490 kilometres (2,790 miles)

Atlantic Intracostal Waterway,* east coast of United States — 3,057 kilometres (1,900 miles)

Damodar Valley Canals, India — 2,494 kilometres (1,550 miles)

Gulf Intracoastal Waterway,* U.S. — 1,770 kilometres (1,100 miles)

Grand Canal, China — 1,747 kilometres (1,086 miles)

Erie Canal, New York, USA — 584 kilometres (363 miles)

This diagram compares the lengths of the world's major canal systems.

* An intracoastal canal runs alongside the coast, slightly inland. It allows ships to travel along the coast without having to deal with tides, currents, and bad weather.

Major ship canals

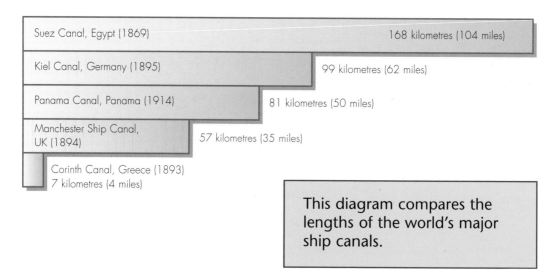

Suez Canal, Egypt (1869) — 168 kilometres (104 miles)

Kiel Canal, Germany (1895) — 99 kilometres (62 miles)

Panama Canal, Panama (1914) — 81 kilometres (50 miles)

Manchester Ship Canal, UK (1894) — 57 kilometres (35 miles)

Corinth Canal, Greece (1893) — 7 kilometres (4 miles)

This diagram compares the lengths of the world's major ship canals.

Big locks and small

Berendrecht Lock,
Antwerp, Belgium
500 m x 68 m
(1,640 ft x 223 ft)

St Lawrence Seaway, Canada
240 m x 24 m (787 ft x 79 ft)

Mississippi System, United States
363 m x 33 m
(1,190 ft x 108 ft)

Rhine-Danube System, Germany
197 m x 12 m (646 ft x 39 ft)

Narrow Canals, Britain
22 m x 2 m (72 ft x 6.5 ft)

Panama Canal, Panama
300 m x 33 m
(984 ft x 108 ft)

Olympic pool
50 m x 20 m (164 ft x 66 ft)

FACTS ✦ Longest, deepest

- Deepest lock: Zaporozhye Lock, Ukraine – 37.4 metres (123 feet)

- Longest staircase: Tardebigge, Worcester and Birmingham Canal, England – 30 locks

- Longest **incline**: Ronquières, Belgium – raise: 67 metres (220 feet); length: 11,600 metres (38,038 feet); maximum barge size: 1350 tonnes

- Longest canal tunnel: Rôve, Marseilles–Rhône, France – length: 7.1 kilometres (4.4 miles)

This diagram shows the biggest and smallest canal locks compared to an Olympic swimming pool.

A freighter steams down the St Lawrence Seaway, North America's most important artificial waterway. It connects Lake Ontario with Montreal and the Atlantic Ocean.

Glossary

alloy material made of a metal combined with another metal or other substance. For example, steel is an alloy made of iron and a small amount of carbon.

aqueduct channel that carries water. The channel may be made of pipes, tunnels and bridges. The word aqueduct is also used for a bridge that carries water.

Assyria ancient empire that flourished in the first millennium BC in the area known today as the Middle East.

bank side of a canal channel or river

barge cargo craft designed for use on canals and waterways

bed bottom of a canal channel or river

bitumen sticky, tar-like substance which is made from oil

blasting breaking up rock using explosives

borehole deep, narrow hole bored down into the ground to take samples of the earth and rocks below

cement mixture of materials that hardens into a rock-like substance after it is mixed with water. Cement is used to make concrete.

contour line drawn on a map that links places on the ground that are all at the same height above sea level

cutting small artificial valley cut through a hill

decade ten years

draught distance from the bottom of a ship's hull to the surface of the water

dredger machine that digs sediment from the bottom of a canal or river. Some dredgers use buckets on a chain; others suck the sediment up through a huge tube.

embankment bank with a flat top and sloping sides. It is built by piling up earth and rock

engineer a person who designs or builds structures

erosion process of water and wind wearing away the rocks of the Earth's surface. Erosion can also wear away canal banks.

hydro-electric power power, normally in the form of electricity, made by letting water from a reservoir flow through a turbine. A generator attached to the turbine creates electricity.

inclined plane sloping track along which canal boats are pulled in large tanks of water

Industrial Revolution   period in history from about 1750 to about 1850 when industries such as iron-making began

in situ   on site; in its final place

irrigation   collecting water and making it flow to where it is needed to water growing crops

isthmus   narrow strip of land connecting two latger land areas

lock   step on a canal which allows ships to move uphill and downhill

Mesopotamia   the ancient name of a region made up of most of modern-day Iraq and parts of Syria and Turkey

Middle East   area of the world made up of north-east Africa and south-west Asia

navigable   suitable for boats or ships to travel along

parasite   animal or plant that lives on another animal and feeds on it

pile   long steel or concrete pole driven deep into the ground

pilot   person who takes charge of a ship to navigate it through difficult areas of ocean or waterway

polythene   floppy plastic that can be made into very thin sheets

precast concrete   concrete that is set into a shape before it is put in place

reinforced concrete   concrete that contains steel reinforcing bars

reservoir   artificial lake formed behind a dam

sediment   material made up from small particles of sand, mud, and plant remains that is washed along a river and settles to the bottom

silt   very fine soil washed down a river and deposited at its mouth

sluice gates   gates that open to allow water to flow into or out of a lock

survey   to measure the ground so that something can be built on it

towpath   path along the bank of a canal. It is called a towpath because barges used to be towed by horses walking along it.

transit   travel through a canal from one end to the other

trapezium   four-sided shape which has two sides of different lengths and two parallel sides

vertical   upright, straight up and down

weir   low dam across a river that creates a deep pool on the upstream side. Water can flow over the top of a weir.

Index

aqueducts 4, 6, 8, 9, 10, 11, 14, 15, 25

banks 8, 10, 17, 18, 20, 21, 27
  erosion 8, 20
barge canals 5, 15
barges 5, 7, 17, 20, 24, 27
  dumb barges 20
  narrow boats 7, 20
bed 8, 10, 18
Berendrecht Lock 5, 29
blasting 17
boreholes 15
bridges 4, 15

canal craft 4, 20
canal design 14–15
Canal du Midi 6
canal lifts 13, 15
canalization 17
cargo transport 5, 6, 7
channel linings 8, 10, 11, 18
channel shapes 8
channel width and depth 15, 23
concrete 8, 9, 10, 11, 18, 19
construction project 16–19
  problems 26–7
cuttings 9, 17, 26, 27

dangers 27
drainage 5
dredgers 21, 23

earth-moving 16, 17, 18, 19, 23
embankments 9, 17
Erie Canal 24–5, 27, 28
excavators 17

Grand Canal, China 5, 6, 7, 28

history of canal building 6–7
hydro-electric power 27

ice-breaking craft 21
inclined planes 13, 15, 29
irrigation 5, 6, 23

Kiel Canal 28

leisure facilities 21, 24, 27
locks 5, 6, 8, 9, 10, 11, 12–13, 14, 15,
  19, 20, 25, 27, 29
lock gates 9, 12, 13, 19, 21
lock staircases 13, 29
longest canal systems 28

Main-Danube Canal 18
maintenance 21
Manchester Ship Canal 28
Marne-Rhine Canal 13
materials 10–11
Mississippi System 20, 28

navigable rivers 17

Panama Canal 4, 7, 12, 19, 26–7, 28, 29
passing places 22
piles 19

Regent's Canal 7
Rhine-Danube System 29
route planning 14, 15

St Lawrence Seaway 24, 29
sea lampreys 25
ship canals 5, 7, 15, 22–3, 26, 28
silt 21, 23
site preparation 16–17
sluice gates 12
speed limits 20
steel 8, 9, 10, 11, 16, 19
Suez Canal 5, 7, 15, 19, 22–3, 27, 28
surveying 16

towpaths 21
tunnels 4, 6, 9, 14, 15, 17, 29

water levels 9, 12, 21
water supply 5, 6
waterproofing 10, 18
waterway networks 5
weirs 17, 27